Beautiful
Wedding Receptions

By Donna Kooler

A LEISURE ARTS PUBLICATION

10   9   8   7   6   5   4   3   2

Library of Congress Cataloging-in-Publication Data
    Kooler, Donna
    Beautiful Wedding Receptions
    "A Leisure Arts Publication"

ISBN: 1-57486-208-1

Contributors

PRODUCED BY

PUBLISHED BY

If you have questions or comments
please contact:

LEISURE ARTS CUSTOMER SERVICE

P.O. Box 55595

Little Rock, AR 72215-9633

www.leisurearts.com

KOOLER DESIGN STUDIO, INC.

399 Taylor Blvd. Suite 104

Pleasant Hill, CA 94523

kds@koolerdesign.com

COLOR SEPARATIONS AND DIGITAL PREPRESS

ADMAC Digital Imaging, Emeryville, CA

Camera Graphics, Lafayette, CA

PRINTED IN THE U.S.A. BY

R.R. Donnelley & Sons, Co.

KOOLER DESIGN STUDIO

PRESIDENT: Donna Kooler
EXECUTIVE V.P.: Linda Gillum
VICE PRESIDENT: Priscilla Timm
EDITOR: Judy Swager
ILLUSTRATORS: Linda Gillum, Barbara Baatz
Sandy Orton, Tom Taneyhill
Nancy Rossi, Jorja Hernandez
STAFF: Sara Angle, Jennifer Drake
Virginia Hanley-Rivett
Marsha Hinkson, Arlis Johnson
Karen Million, Char Randolph

ELEGANT WEDDING CEREMONIES

CREATIVE DIRECTOR: Donna Kooler
BOOK DESIGN: Nancy Wong Spindler
WRITERS: Kit Schlich, Shelley Carda
Joanne Lehrer
COPY EDITORS: Joan Cravens, Judy Swager
ILLUSTRATORS: Linda Gillum, Sandy Orton
PHOTOGRAPHERS: Dianne Woods, Berkeley, CA
Don Fraser, Berkeley, CA
PHOTO STYLISTS: Donna Kooler, Basha Hanner
Ina Rice
SUPPORT: Darlene Barrett-Garrahan
Q. Stone Forbess, Laurie Grant
Deborah Magers-Rankin

Contents

The Wedding Reception Of Your Dreams

YOUR WEDDING RECEPTION WILL BE THE PARTY OF YOUR life! It will be a time to celebrate your love by gathering together all the people who are meaningful to you and your new husband. To this you add the refreshment of food and drink and the opportunity to offer toasts, dance, and mingle with guests.

If you love to throw parties, you are sure to enjoy planning and selecting all the elements that will make your reception memorable. If you feel inexperienced or uncomfortable about entertaining, there are professionals ready to help you make your dreams a reality.

A professional wedding consultant is a tremendous boon if you don't know where or how to begin designing your reception. She (or he) can help you plan and coordinate all aspects of your party, from the champagne to the getaway limousine and everything in between. In addition, the consultant will be there for you on your wedding day, attending to all the elements that are important to you. She is also a good choice to be your director (see next page). If you decide to hire a consultant, seek recommendations from satisfied brides as well as vendors such as bakers, caterers, and florists.

Because your reception will take up the largest amount of your wedding budget, it is the area where you can save (or spend) the most money and where you can exercise the greatest control over what you spend. In this book you will find ideas to help you make the most of your reception budget so you can offer your guests a delightful party and, at the same time, enjoy the reception you have always dreamed about.

Your wedding reception director keeps you informed and your reception running smoothly.

Paramount in your reception planning will be developing a budget you can live with. Knowing the amount you have to spend will free you to make important decisions on the major elements of your reception—the location, flowers, cake, menu, music, and all the delightful personal touches such as favors and decorations. Another good reason to firm up your budget early is that it enables you to proceed with reserving your most desirable reception services. Popular sites, photographers, florists, and bakers are often booked a year in advance.

Your reception will work most smoothly if one person is "in charge." Ironically, as much as you might want to do it yourself, you are not the best choice for this job! Your groom and your guests will want to spend time with you and offer you their good wishes. They will not be able to do so if you are busy directing the caterer, photographer, and other service people. So, elect a director for this important responsibility. Your director might be your wedding consultant, reception coordinator, or a non-professional such as a friend or a family member. (If you choose one of the latter, make sure you thank and reward him or her in a special way, before or after your wedding.)

Work with your director to devise a timeline for your reception activities (see the next chapter) and make a point of introducing your director—preferably before the wedding day—to the various personnel he or she will direct behind the scene.

The site manager or coordinator oversees the physical arrangements such as setting up guest tables and chairs, buffet tables, the dance floor, lighting, and amenities such as coat racks and rest rooms. If your location has no manager, you will need to appoint someone to set things up.

Whatever the surroundings, you can make your reception as formal or informal as you wish.

The florist provides the key elements of décor. Depending on your decorating scheme, you may also need additional personnel to dress things up before the wedding. Enlist friends and family members to help out.

The cake baker, caterer, bartender, and food- and beverage-serving personnel must turn their attention to the reception while you are celebrating your wedding ceremony. It's essential that they have access to the reception site before you arrive.

The bandleader, musicians, disk jockey, or person in charge of taped music will look for guidance in setting the tempo of the reception.

The photographer and videographer, whether professional or non-professional, need to know where and when significant events such as cake cutting and the first dance will occur. They should also be encouraged to record personal and impromptu moments.

Now, wouldn't you rather have someone else attend to all these details? You deserve to savor each special moment, receive your guests' good wishes, smile for the camera, dance as if you had not a care in the world, and linger in conversation with those who love you. It's your day to shine! ✄

Designing Your Reception

A MELLOW AFTERNOON GARDEN PARTY WITH A HARPIST, a sophisticated cocktail party with a jazz trio, a spirited banquet with abundant food and ethnic music—what scenario tickles your fancy? How do you envision this most joyous of celebrations, your wedding reception? Let yourself dream!

Your reception can be lavish or simple, sedate or energetic, and it can take place anytime from dawn till dawn again. It can continue the serene pace of your wedding, or kick up its heels and dance. It can be folk dances passed on for generations or music of a bygone age. You can have the latest jazz band or music from a Renaissance fair. Family, friends, and the music of conversation may be all the heart requires.

You can serve your guests hearty, ethnic dishes and you can let them eat cake. Nothing traditional is ever too humble; nothing the purse permits is too opulent. You feast on your dreams.

Decorations support and extend your fantasies. The great outdoors can be tamed to a bower or taken *al fresco*; the great indoors can be transformed into a tropical paradise. You can have rainbow streamers of silk or the sky beribboned with clouds. The limit is your budget, but your wealth is your imagination.

The newlyweds receive their guests at this outdoor champagne reception.

ORCHESTRATING YOUR RECEPTION

Many brides and grooms organize their reception activities into a structure that has evolved over time. The arrangements and activities listed below have proved popular with generations of newlyweds.

THE RECEIVING LINE is the traditional way for your guests to greet you and your groom as newlyweds. It also allows your friends and family to introduce themselves to each other.

Plan to receive your guests fairly early in the festivities while everyone is still basking in the glow of the ceremony. Ask your immediate family and attendants to join you in a receiving line. It's customary for whomever is hosting the reception (which may or may not be the bride and groom) to head the line.

FOOD AND DRINK are an essential part of the reception, even something as simple as cocktails and hors d'oeuvres. For something more elaborate, choose an informal meal, a lavish buffet, or a seated, multi-course feast. Remember, even cake and punch make a rare feast when offered with grace and a heart full of hospitality.

TOASTS are verbal gifts that make people shout with laughter, weep with sentiment, and recall the joys of their own weddings. Traditionally, the Best Man begins the toasting after dinner, proposing the health of the bride and groom. Next, the couple toast their parents and each other, and then the father of the bride offers his toast. After that, it is a free-for-all of blessings. But toasts can be offered at the beginning of dinner to the health of the guests, or by a mother welcoming all to share in her joy. Kind words are always welcome. Even if you don't plan on videotaping your entire wedding and reception, consider making a tape of these moments to savor later.

THE FIRST DANCE is reserved for the newlyweds, though sometimes the father dances with the bride first, and reluctantly releases her to her new husband. If not, it is customary for the father to have the next dance with his daughter, while the groom dances with his mother. Then the bride and groom may dance with their new in-laws, and then guests at large. Any special song for this first dance should be specified to the musicians when they are hired. It may run the gamut from romantic ball-room dancing to folk dancing to the latest popular step.

If you select music for a traditional ballroom number but don't know the steps, learn them well before your wedding. If you don't wish to dance, select an alternate musical offering: a special song performed for the bride and groom, or a group sing-along as guests hold hands in a circle around the newlyweds.

Whether a centuries-old folk dance (above) or a musical embrace (below), the first dance always draws the guests onto the dance floor.

The guest book (above) records the names—and often the congratulations—of the wedding guests for posterity.

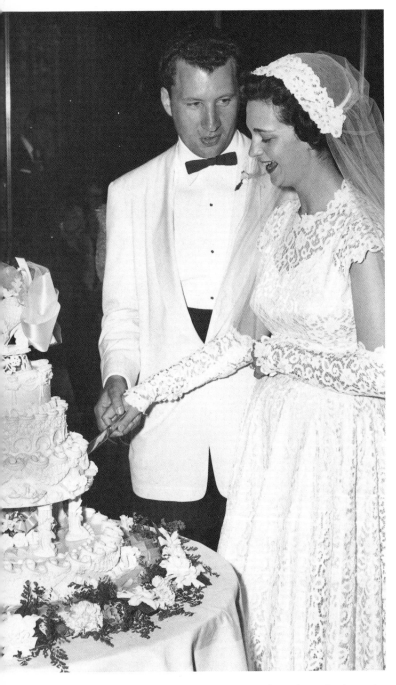

Donna and Douglas Kooler enjoy the traditional cake-cutting ceremony during their wedding reception in 1954.

CUTTING THE CAKE has become almost as significant as the exchange of rings during the ceremony. It is the first duty that the newlyweds perform as a couple, and serving each other a bit of cake symbolizes their willingness to nurture each other during their lives together.

To follow traditional protocol, the bride picks up the knife with her right hand and the groom places his hand atop hers. They make two cuts for the first slice, then put the cake on a plate. They feed each other a bite of cake—the groom feeds the bride, then the bride the groom. Next, they cut slices for their parents; the bride serves the groom's parents, and the groom hers. The caterer then steps in to cut the cake and serve the rest of the guests.

WEDDING FAVORS are delightful, small gifts for your guests. They're so much fun, they deserve their own chapter (see page 57).

There is great excitement and fun (above) as the single ladies try to catch the bride's bouquet.
This couple (right) found a clever way to exit the festivities.

TOSSING THE BRIDE'S BOUQUET is a fun, sentimental crowd-pleaser because legend has it that whoever catches the bouquet will be the next bride in your circle of friends and relations. It is optional, however. Some brides elect to keep the bouquet as a memento or to present it to a grandmother or other significant woman in the bride's life. They toss a second bouquet to the unmarried women who wish to participate.

THE GETAWAY is the last reception event for the newlyweds. For those who want to leave with a flourish, tributes such as the tossing of birdseed, the ringing of bells, or the blowing of bubbles—if not expressed immediately after the ceremony—are appropriate at this time. (For three lovely project ideas, see our companion book, *Elegant Wedding Ceremonies*.) This grand send-off is optional, of course. Many couples elect to stay until the end of the party.

This perfect outdoor setting needs no extra decoration. The lush greenery forms a graceful arch above the bride and her guests.

WHERE TO CELEBRATE

The location you choose for your reception will influence the look and ambiance of your party. As you begin your search for the perfect spot, balance these intangibles with practicality, weighing the atmosphere of the site against such things as the comfort of your guests and the ease of operation for your caterer and other service personnel.

Popular sites are often booked up to a year in advance, especially for the summer months, so this is a decision you will want to make as soon as you choose the actual wedding date, or perhaps even before. Sites to consider include restaurants, hotels, clubs, country inns, wineries, a church

or synagogue hall, or a private residence. For all but the last, ask to speak to the site coordinator or manager.

In your search, ask practical questions such as:

❧ Is the size of the facility appropriate for the number of reception guests you have in mind—neither too large nor too small?

❧ Are there enough tables and chairs, or will you have to rent them?

❧ Are the kitchen facilities, parking, and rest rooms adequate for the size of reception you envision? Will the site require valet parking service?

❧ Can the site accommodate guests with special needs, such as someone in a wheelchair? Is there a diaper-changing area for guests with babies?

❧ Are the lighting and power sources sufficient for your photographer, videographer, bandleader, or disk jockey? Are they easily accessible?

❧ Will you be able to book the site for only a short window of time? What if your reception lasts longer than you originally envision?

❧ Does the site offer a package of services including catering, bartender, decorations, music, and a coordinator? How does the price compare to securing these services on your own?

Make sure you know exactly, in writing, what services you will receive, including the number of serving personnel, extra fees such as cake-cutting charges, and hidden costs such as wine corkage fees.

A PRIVATE HOME reception allows you to entertain your guests in greater intimacy. If you choose this option, be sure to select a reception director so you won't find yourself on the spot, directing the activities yourself. If you are planning a catered meal, have prospective caterers evaluate the kitchen before you sign an agreement and make sure they will bring the food completely ready to serve. Your family may offer to prepare the food, but avoid the temptation of over-extending everyone with kitchen tasks; you need to stay fresh for your guests and your groom. A considerate bride will let the neighbors know of the event in advance so they may anticipate the extra traffic and possible noise.

AN OUTDOOR RECEPTION can be formal or casual. It depends mostly on the menu. For any outdoor reception you will need to have furniture, shade, shelter, plumbing, and a kitchen. The shade and shelter can be

The clever use of flowers can turn a swimming pool into an imaginative water garden.

Whatever your outdoor entertaining dreams, just elaborate on the basic requirements of shade, furniture, and lots of cool drinks.

tents or tables with umbrellas, and these may have to be rented, set up, and removed. No matter what you serve, these basics will be the same. You may also want additional table decorations and tulle for chairs.

If you are celebrating your wedding in summer, consider whether you may also need fans to keep your guests comfortable. In hot weather, your guests will probably need more to drink, especially icy non-alcoholic beverages. Evaluate whether your location will require citronella candles to keep an evening reception bug-free.

SERVING YOUR GUESTS

Cake only, a cocktail party, a candlelit dinner—what would you like? Select a menu in keeping with the mood of your wedding, the location, and your preferences. If you're getting married in the parlor of a romantic bed and breakfast inn, you may want to provide a lavish breakfast spread. Springtime in a friend's garden? A filling lunch salad sprinkled with edible flowers is just the thing. If you are holding your reception at a place without a commercial kitchen, such as a beach cottage, or with an unusual feature such as an antique stove, be sure to tell your caterers so they can do their best for you. They'll need to know whether to bring extra worktables, or if their oversized trays will fit inside the oven.

Catering may well be your single biggest wedding expense. It's also where you can save the most money. Do you save more with a sit-down dinner or with a buffet? Service tends to cost more with a sit-down dinner, but guests at a buffet eat more, adding to the food costs. Much depends on the individual caterer's experience, so ask your caterer about what he or she specializes in. Or consider a compromise between a sit-down meal and a buffet: serve the salad and cake at the table, but offer the entrée as a buffet.

If you will be delayed taking photographs or greeting guests in a receiving line, serve hungry guests appetizers as they wait for you (and skip the appetizer at the table). Choosing either soup or salad, but not both, is also a good way to keep costs down. Each choice of entrée adds to the total cost of your reception, so rather than have several choices, offer just one or two. Include a vegetarian option as well, because more and more people are vegetarians these days.

Liquor, if you choose to serve it, is a significant cost as well. Champagne is a wedding classic, but sparkling wine or prosecco, a light, bubbly wine, are festive, too. A great money-saving trick is to ask your caterer to pass a "house cocktail" to everyone at the beginning of the reception, then continue to serve it throughout. Kir Royale (champagne and cassis) or Bellini (fresh peach puree and sparkling wine) are festive and not too high in alcohol. Your caterer can serve these along with beer, wine, and soft drinks.

Hiring a professional bartender is a good idea if you decide to serve liquor at your reception. Although it may seem more economical to ask a friend or relative, a professional is used to serving large numbers of people quickly and will be better with portion control, resulting in less waste.

If your reception is at a hotel or restaurant that provides bartender service, you can choose a dollar limit ($500 or $1000, for example) and have the bar quietly close after the limit is reached or switch to serving non-alcoholic beverages.

An espresso cart provides festive coffees, teas, and Italian sodas to your guests who don't drink alcohol.

WHAT TIME TO CELEBRATE

When selecting the time of day for your reception, it will help you to know that generally as the day progresses, so does the formality of your wedding meal. A wedding breakfast is usually more casual than a midnight dessert buffet and champagne bar. As the day progresses, the cost of the reception will rise.

Intangibles count; you and your groom may already have a favorite time of day in mind. Perhaps you love the quality of light in a particular setting at a certain hour. Your guests are sure to enjoy it too. ᴈ

Lavish bouquets can turn a simple table into a landscape.

SAMPLE MENUS

BREAKFAST OR BRUNCH

A delightful complement to a mid- or late-morning wedding, a reception featuring breakfast or brunch is a treat for a bride and groom (and their guests) who plan on traveling later in the day. A reception at this time of day can save you money because it is the least expensive full-meal option and guests usually drink more sparingly at this time. Coffee, tea, and champagne, or champagne-based cocktails such as mimosa or Bellini, are appropriate for a breakfast or brunch reception.

Bellini or mimosa
Fresh fruit platter
Assorted pastries: maple pecan muffins, brioche,
pain au chocolat, and ginger scones
Crustless quiche with smoked salmon,
dill, and sour cream
Almond-apricot coffee cake
Coffee, tea, hot chocolate made with white chocolate

LUNCHEON

Served between 12:00 noon and 2:00 p.m., lunch follows a late morning or high noon wedding and offers you menu options. You might serve a full meal, either table service or buffet, or choose a substantial salad such as curried chicken, spring lamb and bitter greens, or duck and wild rice. With soup or a selection of appetizers and wedding cake, your guests will feel well-cared for, and you won't break the bank.

Cocktail of prosecco and lime
Gazpacho
Assorted breads
Salad of grilled chicken breast, heirloom tomatoes, and
mozzarella, drizzled with pesto
Chocolate wedding cake filled with raspberries
and whipped cream
Coffee, tea

TEA

Customarily served between 2:00 and 5:00 p.m., this or the cocktail reception is the easiest to manage if you're planning on doing your own catering. Traditionally, your menu would include champagne, tea sandwiches, scones with jam, lemon curd, and clotted cream, wedding cake, and an assortment of teas.

Champagne
Bread-and-butter anchovy pinwheels
Watercress and cucumber sandwiches
Scones with clotted cream and jam
Assorted fruit dipped in chocolate
White cake filled with strawberries and
frosted with buttercream
China tea

SAMPLE MENUS

COCKTAILS

Beginning between 4:00 and 7:30 p.m., a cocktail reception in late afternoon usually features light hors d'oeuvres. At an early evening reception, plan to serve something a bit more substantial because it's closer to dinner time. Consider skewers of chicken, prosciutto and figs, or warm feta and spinach turnovers. Depending on the reception length, count on five to six hors d'oeuvres for each guest.

Red and white wine,
beer and soft drinks or full bar
Bruschetta with wild mushrooms, asparagus frittata,
Thinly sliced beef medallions on crostini
with gorgonzola butter,
Polenta pizza with eggplant and peppers
Red pepper hummus on endive
Crocombouche
Coffee

DINNER

Served between 5:00 and 9:00 p.m., dinners may vary greatly in menu and luxury. Dinners are generally the most expensive meal option, too, but you can control the price of each serving by the foods you choose. Beef tenderloin appears expensive, but there is little waste and portions can be closely monitored, so it ends up being more cost-effective than you might think. A game hen costs no more than the usual chicken but has great eye appeal. Whole portobello mushrooms are a rich-tasting vegetarian option.

Kir Royale
Butter lettuce and avocado with citrus vinaigrette
Game hen with couscous stuffing
or stuffed portobello mushroom
Broccoli and red pepper sauté
White cake filled with fresh peaches and
topped with rolled marzipan
Espresso cart

EVENING BUFFET

Usually served after the dinner hour, from about 7:00 p.m. until midnight, this is a newly popular option for a late-night party. The evening buffet is a lovely choice for a Christmas, New Year's Eve, or Valentine's Day wedding or a Friday or Saturday evening. Finger food and cookies are pleasing treats for nibbling. Want that show-stopping wedding cake? Here's your chance.

Rosé champagne
Caviar on toast points
Savory almond-custard tartlets
Smoked turkey on black bread
Mexican wedding cookies, chocolate chip cookies,
biscotti, cinnamon shortbread
Warm crepes Suzette
Chocolate espresso torte with whipped cream
Espresso cart

Wedding Cakes

BREAD IS THE STAFF OF LIFE, BUT WHEN WE CELEBRATE THE sweetness of life, we eat cake. Cake is not the food of sadness or hard times. Cake is made of the foods of good fortune—sweet butter, sugar, ripe fruits, and the finest flour—and is a symbol of abundance. Eat bread for the simple joy of being alive, but for the joining of two lives, only cake will do. A wedding must be celebrated with cake.

And we love our wedding cakes. We love them so much that we have stately cake rituals. We bake trinkets in them for good luck. We cover them with flowers and fruits and all the beautiful things that we can think of to represent sweetness. We crown them with statues that we keep forever and pass on to our heirs, to remind us of the joy of love. We have ceremonies where we photograph the cake and then the cutting of it using gleaming swords or beautiful silver knives. We watch the bride and groom feed each other cake, to show how they will nurture each other with love's sweetness. We feast upon the bridal cake ourselves, to partake of their happiness. We put cake into tiny boxes tied with satin ribbons, and we take it home and sleep upon it, because sleeping on the cake will bring us sweet dreams of love. We love our cakes. And we share our cakes with love.

STRUCTURE OF LAYERS
AND FILLINGS

When you choose a wedding cake, you need to consider the structural potential of desserts. Originally, pound cakes and fruitcakes were the basic big wedding cakes because they were dense and durable. Then chemistry gave us dependable leavenings, and light, fluffy cakes became the norm. This presents problems when you want an architectural, multi-tiered confection.

Butter cake is also dense. Its fine grain contains little air in the spaces, making it a dandy cake for a real edifice of dessert. Sponge cake is airier. Beaten eggs trap air, which produces volume. The eggs give elasticity and resilience, so the cake is lighter.

If you want a tiered cake, layer directly upon layer, use a really solid cake or reinforcing supports. A fine example is the Rose Adagio cake (opposite). The tower of layer upon layer demands a butter cake to prevent flattening. It also needs a solid filling which will stay in place. This cake has a buttercream frosting as a filling, but marzipan, fondant, or a solid fruit curd or ganache would be as effective.

If you want an open-tiered cake, you will have to use supports, generally attractive little columns with dowel rods inserted into the cake beneath. This is how to engineer tiers. The same heavy butter cake, Rose Adagio, is magically engineered (right) into a tall, graceful cake with flowers between the tiers.

If you have decided to have a series of tiers with completely different cakes and fillings, you can engineer the tiers and decorate all the different cakes to look alike, as we have done with the beautiful Flower Basket cakes on page 26–27. But what if you want to emphasize the differences? Perhaps you want a butter cake with marzipan filling for the bottom tier, a chocolate Génoise filled with light ganache for the middle tier, and a light, whipped cream filling in a lemon sponge cake for the top tier. Then, you could break the single tower of cake into a neighborhood of several cakes, flavors, and choices for

wildly successful and surprising strawberry shortcake on page 29. The sliced berries, marinated in rosé and sugar, were well drained and placed on frozen sponge layers. Then the strawberries were covered with stabilized whipped cream, the layers stacked into tiers held in place with paper collars, and chilled until firm. Finally, the tiers were slathered with stabilized whipped cream frosting and chilled until the wedding began.

While the wedding was in progress, the whole cake was assembled with supports, decorated with piped cream and fresh flowers, and wheeled into the reception just before the guests arrived. Naturally, the photographs of the bridal party were taken *before* this wedding. You can get away with something this daring if you adhere strictly to schedule.

Vertical design is not the only consideration in a wedding cake. Sometimes the shape needs a little embellishment, or sometimes a special decoration is showcased. Even a tiny cake for an intimate wedding can be impressive. On pages 32–33 a nut torte has been fashioned into an exotic swirl by just trimming one wing off of a standard heart-shaped cake. This allows you to nestle an heirloom statue into the cake or accentuate it using fragrant roses tucked in at the base.

The same heart shape (page 36) can be artfully decorated using fondant coating tinged with rose to imitate marble. The light-hearted Biscuit de Savoie within is layered with a rich and sophisticated rum cream. The exquisite flowers also hide a surprise: they are fondant accented by artificial leaves.

If you wish to take a light cake to great heights, you can do it using thin layers or stiff fillings or both. The sponge cake (page 37, top left) has been sliced into six thin layers, separated by coconut cream and pineapple, guava, lime, and passion fruit curds. The whole was iced with whipped cream and crowned with orchids, in keeping with its tropical fillings.

Whatever your options, you won't go wrong if you stick to the classics. The true nobility of a humble grocery

your guests. This makes it easier to serve different flavors to the people who want them.

Frosting also adds weight, and with a cake such as the mammoth tower on page 28, (also see cakes on pages 35 top and bottom right, and 37 top right) fondant frosting and long, beautiful fondant streamers may be too heavy for a light sponge cake and fillings. If you are going to have a frosting heavy enough to roll out, choose a cake and filling which will support it, especially on the large lower tiers.

You can sometimes assemble a large cake with light fillings and layers at the last minute. Such a cake was the

store cake (page 38) is revealed like Cinderella at the ball when transformed with roses from the floral department. Classic white butter cake and buttercream frosting live happily ever after.

Traditions revolving around the cake are sacrosanct. Cake is what people think of when you say "wedding reception." People will remember that you cut a cake, and served cake. How far this can be from actual cake is ticklish. Your parents and their friends will expect a wedding cake that looks and tastes like a wedding cake. Some possible variations are petits fours and cupcakes, and we will talk of these later.

TRADITIONAL CAKES

Traditional cakes fall into three principal categories: butter cakes, sponge cakes, and tea cakes. Classic wedding cakes (buttercakes) come in yellow or the more traditional white. They are rich, light, fragrant, have a fine crumb, and blend beautifully with flavorings, interesting fillings, and toppings. They are also sturdy, which is of paramount importance if you are having the cake carried to some remote reception site, or if you want a wedding cake with multiple tiers. They are superb for afternoon tea receptions because they are rich and satisfying.

Sponge cakes are airy, drier, lighter than butter cakes, and very versatile. They are made light by eggs, so they soak up liqueurs and syrups beautifully, retaining the exquisite flavors without becoming gummy. Sponge cakes also come in an amazing number of variations, such as rich chocolate, almond, and hazelnut. If you want petits fours, sponge cake is a good base. After a substantial dinner, light sponge cake will be appreciated.

Tea cakes can serve as wedding cakes. They are loved for their pronounced and distinct flavors. Pound cake, carrot cake, poppy seed cake, and peel cakes are the best known examples. They are perfect for wedding breakfasts, when guests may prefer to avoid heavily sugared frosting.

Someone else's tradition is always fun. There are lots of different kinds of wedding cakes if you look far enough. One type that is becoming popular in the United States is the French wedding Croquembouche. These are little choux pastry puffs with a classic crème filling, stacked and glued together into a huge tower using caramelized sugar. This is disassembled and offered to the guests, generally two puffs per serving.

The puffs are extremely simple to make and fill, and they can be augmented with a fresh strawberry or raspberry along with the crème filling. Practice adhering them together, so they will stay that way until serving time, or you can find a pastry chef to do it for you.

Petits fours (page 30, right) are delightful and traditional at weddings, but they tend to be invisible as the main dessert, probably because there is no ceremony surrounding them, and no real sharing, as with traditional cakes. They can be expensive too, so check with your cake baker about quantity and cost.

A tower of never-ending delight...(page 31, left) Delectible tidbits of choux puffs, miniature white or chocolate brownies, rugalach, and chocolate-dipped staw-berries not only offer your guests the luxury of choice but the appearance of endless abundance. As guests remove individual pieces, the caterer (or other helper) refills the display from a secret supply below the table, so the tower never diminishes.

Cupcakes (page 31, right) are not traditional, though they are certainly cake, and they are a blessing at garden and outdoor weddings and where there are lots of children. You can cut your ceremonial cake and then bring out the cupcake reinforcements, which can be as delicious as the official cake.

Sprinkle cupcakes with an infinite variety of syrups and liqueurs, fill them with fabulous fillings, frost them with a rainbow of icings, and have a wonderful time doing it. If you want a really unusual cake to serve to your adult guests, you might make cupcakes which look like the wedding cake, but are actually more palatable to children.

FILLINGS

Fillings are a delight because they surprise you, perhaps with a ribbon of mellow crushed almonds in a rich chocolate Génoise or a bright, tart lime curd hiding in a layer of butter cake.

Fruit fillings are always popular. The refreshing tang of fruit is a delightful contrast to butter cakes with butter-cream frostings, and it is equally at home in a simple sponge cake with vanilla sugar sprinkled on top. When deciding on a fruit filling, consider the flavors of the other

components of the cake and whether you wish to contrast with them or to support them. An orange marmalade filling in a light carrot cake is a tangy flavor contrast which enhances the color, while a lemon curd in a lemon sponge cake underscores the lemon flavor in the layers.

Jellies, jams, and marmalades are ideal for thin layers of filling, even when mixed and layered with each other or with cream fillings. Curds are a thick jelly made with butter and egg yolks. Citrus curds are the most commonly used, because of their bright clarity, but berry, passion fruit, guava, and other exotic curds are also possible. They are delightful when enhanced with a complementary syrup sprinkled on the cake, and they are well-suited to hot weather.

Especially good in a chilly season, custards and creams are rich and soothing. The range of tastes is almost limitless, with cream carrying even the most delicate rose or orange flavors so that they are not lost in the richness of a butter cake. Cakes with cream or custard fillings are popular with just about everybody, and they are very satisfying if you are serving a light dinner.

Crushed nut fillings are a good choice for cakes which are not sweet, but should be rich. Marzipan is a ready-made almond paste, equally at home in the most intense chocolate or the mildest almond sponge. Nut pastes and creams have subtle, sophisticated flavors most adults love.

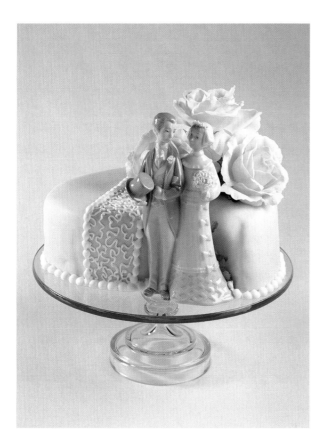

Consider the season when choosing a cake filling or frosting. A fragile mousse filling may collapse in July. If it is going to be hot, outdoors or in, choose something other than custard that needn't be chilled. Fruit curds, sliced marinated fruits, or jellies and jams are a good choice if you want something other than frosting filling. Chocolate truffle fillings, marzipan and other nut-based fillings are also tasty and stable.

TOPPING IT ALL OFF

Frosting and decoration for your cake, much like your wedding dress, are matters of taste and style, and they offer lots of opportunities for delicious experimentation. Once you know the kind of cake you want, it is time to think about covering it up. Here are some basics.

Flavorings, liqueurs, and extracts give cakes and frostings character. These liquids have a high alcohol content, the result of the way the flavor is extracted and preserved. You can use extracts and liqueurs the same way you use vanilla (the most famous extract of them all), and in more ways. In addition to adding a subtle fragrance or flavor to a frosting, you can determine the entire character of the dessert, from the inside out. Sugar syrups with a few teaspoons of a liqueur mixed in, then sprinkled on a sponge cake, set the flavor tone of the whole pastry.

There are far more flavors than vanilla, almond, and chocolate. For every fruit there is a liqueur, and probably more than one. Chambord raspberry liqueur added to whipped cream imparts a fragrance that is absolutely unsurpassed. Or add it to unsalted butter for a delicious wedding breakfast spread. Use it in a frosting or a filling for cream puffs or cupcakes.

A dollop of Grand Marnier during the making will have people swooning over their truffles. Vandermint turns instant cocoa into the Rembrandt of hot chocolates. But don't stop there. Investigate the liqueurs from your favorite fruits and flavors, even chocolate. You will

The groom's contribution to the reception goodies has traditionally been a fruitcake, cut and boxed and sent home with the guests to give them dreams of love. But you don't have to waste a perfectly good opportunity to indulge in sweet dreams. Whatever cake the groom chooses is the groom's cake: raspberry mousse cake, mom's apple pie, or truffle torte as rich as a ransom. If it looks just too good to sleep on, devour it on the spot and have a good time doing it.

find a dozen things that will broaden and enliven your culinary horizons.

Extracts are found in the baking aisle of the grocery. Choose only pure extracts, not artificial ones because artificial flavors degrade under the heat of baking.

There are also flower waters, which are flower oils suspended in water, rather than alcohol. Orange flower water and rosewater are the best known, but there are also lilac waters, frangipani waters, jasmine waters, and probably many others to be discovered. These can be used in baking, though heat drives off the delicate flavor. They are excellent when mixed into cool sugar syrup and sprinkled on a sponge cake. They also can be blended into fondants and frostings for an indescribably delicate taste of flowers. Flower waters can be found at the occasional drug store and from some on-line and mail order cooking supply stores. You may even find them in your friendly neighborhood grocery.

FROSTINGS AND THEIR FRIENDS

Buttercream, the time-honored wedding cake frosting, is made of sugar, butter, and flavorings and is often used on butter cakes. Pure extracts of chocolate, vanilla, orange, almond, or lemon are tasty additions, as are espresso or coconut. Puréed berries are sometimes used, but can make a frosting watery. You are better off layering a butter cream with a curd or jam. This approach gives a wonderful chance to have beautifully striped fillings, which can be much admired once the cake is cut.

Royal frosting is a variety of buttercream that is fortified with meringue powder, to stiffen it nicely after it has set a bit. This is a good base for heavy decorations such as ceramic statuettes or bouquets of real or frosting flowers. It is sturdy and will transport well. And if you want frosting roses for the children to take home, royal frosting is the one to use.

Whipped cream, often stabilized with a little gelatin, makes a rich frosting which is perfect for air-conditioned reception halls or winter. It is a wonderfully delicate frosting, but it mars easily, so it is not really good for transporting, and it may collapse in very hot weather. From fragrant fillings to soft, velvety frostings, whipped cream is so beautiful and versatile, though, that it is worth its weight in trouble.

Fondant is a smooth, dense frosting made of sugar, water, and corn syrup kneaded into a paste. Fondant is rolled flat, fitted over the cake, and trimmed. It is also formed into incredibly realistic flowers and ribbons, and in skilled hands it produces cakes that are as beautiful as museum porcelains. If you opt for a fondant-covered cake, ask your photographer to capture it on film before you slice it. You are sure to want a special photo in your wedding album.

Ganache, a blend of chocolate and cream, usually with a bit of butter or a touch of corn syrup added to make it shiny, is poured over the cake for a smooth, satiny look. Ganache is sometimes flavored with fruit liqueurs. This is a very intense frosting, best avoided on extremely sweet cakes. It is superb with sponge cakes and nuts, and it is a very good filling if you want a rich wedding torte. For an ivory-colored cake, use white chocolate. Use a true white chocolate, such as Lindt brand, which contains real cocoa butter; avoid the artificially flavored "pastel coating" sometimes misleadingly sold as white chocolate.

Marzipan is made of almond paste, sugar, and a bit of corn syrup, like fondant, but it has a grainy texture. It can be rolled and shaped like fondant, and it makes a delicious frosting, filling, or decoration and is practically heat proof.

The perfect pairing does not come from a book. If you want to sample frostings and cakes together, go to a bakery and check out the cupcakes. If you tell the baker you are looking for a wedding cake and testing flavor combinations, he or she may even make up cupcakes specially, so that you can try them out. If the bakery is famous for wedding cakes, ask if they will make you a sample of some specific combination the next time they make it up as a

wedding cake. Many pastry chefs are glad to help a bride choose something unusual and fun.

Decorations for your cake are as individual as you are. Fresh flowers are always lovely, but be careful which fresh flowers you choose. Some of them are poisonous, so check with the florist first if you want fresh flowers. Silk flowers, edible blossoms, and ribbons, real or confectionery, are just a few of the trims to consider. Perhaps you will want a classic bride-and-groom cake topper, or fondant flowers to match your bouquets. You may want delicate lace or embroidery rendered in frosting. Review your baker's portfolio for ideas, and let your fancy lead you where it will.

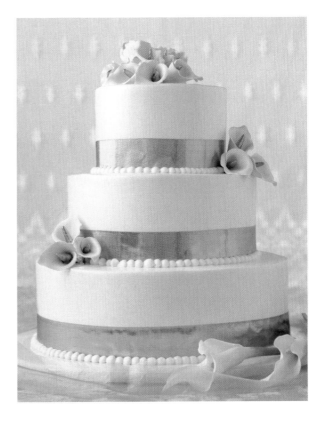

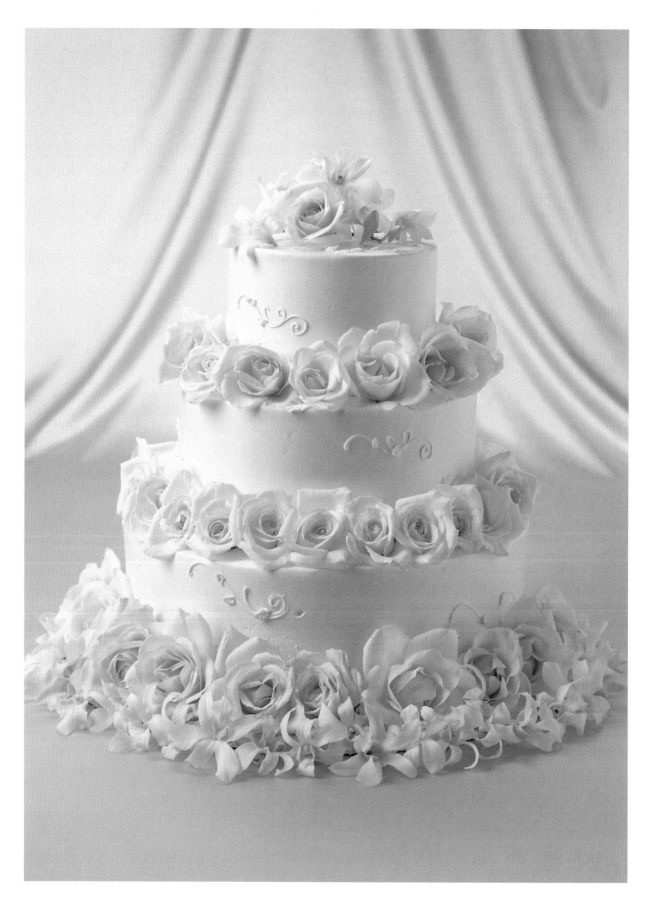

ORDERING YOUR CAKE

Ah, the cake—the *piece de resistance* of the wedding reception! It is so important that you will probably begin thinking about it almost as soon as you begin planning your ceremony. Selecting your cake, and the person who will create it, is a thrilling task because, like your gown, your cake is an expression of your personal style.

Cake bakers, like dress designers, are creative artists, often specializing in particular types of confectionery treats. One might be known for elegant, traditional French Croquembouche, while another makes yummy all-American chocolate buttermilk cake and a third is beloved for sophisticated, fondant-covered layers of liqueur-soaked sponge cake.

Before ordering your cake, gather suggestions from friends and family members and plan to interview several bakers. In addition to the baker who works in a shop, consider a pastry chef, chef's assistant, culinary student, or cooking instructor for the cake of your dreams. Prior to final selection, verify that your reception site will permit you to bring in a cake from your baker of choice. Check local and state regulations, too; some states require food professionals to use certified (inspected) kitchens and carry insurance. You will want to be sure your baker meets all the necessary qualifications.

When you visit potential bakers, review their portfolios. You will enjoy seeing—and they will love showing you—what they can do! Share your ideas for the reception: the location, the anticipated ambiance or style of the party, possible menu, and an estimate of the number of guests. That way, the baker can make suggestions as well as estimate how much cake you will need and the probable cost. Finally, on this first visit, request samples or purchase pieces of cake to take home and taste with your fiancée.

Once you have settled on a baker and shared specific plans for your reception, you can discuss details of cost. Wedding cakes are typically priced by the serving. (You need to have a pretty firm idea at this point of the number of guests.) Don't hesitate to ask about the size of a typical serving and whether you can stretch your cake budget by cutting pieces somewhat smaller. Or perhaps you can serve guests a slice of cake cut from a less expensive but equally delicious sheet cake rather than your showpiece confection. This last suggestion is usually an acceptable option that can save you a great deal of money, particularly if you have your heart set on a cake with fondant or marzipan frosting (which add about 30 percent to your cake costs).

If you have other concerns relating to the cake (guests with special dietary needs, for example), share them with your baker. You'll find that most bakers are eager to work with you, to ensure that your cake truly will be your heart's desire, a masterpiece for your special day.

Decorating Your Reception

ELEGANT, OLD-FASHIONED, EXOTIC—WHATEVER THE STYLE you choose for your reception, the decorations that greet your guests as they arrive for the festivities will put everyone into a party mood. Choose what you love and everything will be fine. You do not have to use what others like. The totality of what you love forms your style the way it forms your personality.

By the time you begin thinking about decorations for your reception, you will already have decided on the season, the hour, and the location for the wedding. Taking these "givens" into consideration, where should you begin planning your reception décor, and how should you go about it?

Start by gathering ideas. In the months preceding the wedding, look for appealing table and room decorations in magazines, decorator showcase homes, department stores, restaurants, clubs, and everywhere else you visit. As you hone your observational skills, you'll find you are defining your preferences as well. You may want to take notes, make sketches, and tear pages out of magazines, noting everything from the colors, linens, and floral arrangements you like best to such small details as the way the napkins are folded and the design of the place cards (in case you decide to use them).

Then, as the day approaches when you start making decisions about your reception décor, you'll be armed with enough information and awareness of your own and the groom's desires that making those decisions will be more fun than confusing. Now, where to begin?

Start at the front door, the entrance to your reception area. A festive, inviting entry, whether in your home, a church reception hall, hotel dining room, or garden, immediately puts guests into the right frame of mind. It sets the tone for the party, extending the romance and the theme or style of your ceremony to the celebration that follows. The rest of the decorations and trims in the room or garden reinforce and enhance the mood.

Table settings, especially if you are planning a sit-down meal rather than a cocktail party, are the biggest single element. Your guests will spend much of their time seated at tables, so focus on table decorations. Do you love the gleam of silver or cut glass? Then include things that reflect light: vases, candelabra, serving dishes, and mirrors. Collect ideas that inspire you, then work with your caterer or reception planner, and create tabletop magic for your own and your guests' enjoyment.

We have assembled four seasonal tables illustrating a few of your many options on pages 43, 45, 47, and 49. Accent colors on the tables—in flowers, napkins, and favors—reflect the colors used in decorations for the ceremony, worn by the bridesmaids, or featured in the wedding flowers.

Spring is abloom on this table (opposite), with a flower-filled compote atop a mat of colorful silk-flower petals. (The mats are easy to make using the instructions on page 55.) Fill the compote with rosebuds cut from short-stemmed blooms; they are more economical than long-stemmed ones. Purchase flowers a few days before the reception, immerse them in water, and allow them to open slightly before the party. Stemmed sherbet glasses, in a delicate hue that complements the flowers, are filled with water and floating tea candles for a flattering, romantic glow. Pale green, lavender-filled sachet bags (favors for guests, see page 76) pick up the green tint in the compote and glasses.
A repeated theme of flowers and fruits turns this table (below) into a garden.

Nature in full bloom creates an easy, comfortable atmosphere which invites the guests to linger.

A small, intimate home reception—tea or cocktail party—allows you to indulge in glorious variety. Amid a host of family pieces, partial sets of dessert plates, and a wealth of mismatched silver, you can create a smorgasbord of color and pattern. Choose linens, candles, and small favors that match a predominant color. For eclectic china and silver, small tables are ideal.

Even if you are having your reception in a hotel, you can still wrap a hotel napkin with a pretty ribbon rose, or gather some Jordan almonds in a square of tulle to tuck into a stemmed glass. Don't be afraid to add colorful table runners to the hotel linens to lend sparkle to a sedate dining room. These special touches make all the difference between *elegant* and *ordinary*.

Summer brings her cool, shady tones to refresh this table (opposite) that features multi-colored hydrangeas tucked into a clear glass vase. (Anchor the stems using glass marbles in colors that match your wedding décor.) Simple white tablecloths from a rental agency are dressed up using colorful handcrafted runners. Pale green napkins are tied using silk-ribbon rose corsages, a lasting memento for guests (see page 72 for instructions).

You don't need a mass of flowers to create visual impact: Romantic softness can be acheived with an elegant minimum.

A few buds, a bit of fern, and candlelight will turn each table into a rose garden.

PLACE CARDS

Will you tell your guests where to sit, or let them seat themselves? The decision rests on your personal preference and the type of reception you are having. At a reception where the guests will be mingling and grazing, such as a tea or a cocktail party, you don't need place cards. But at a sit-down event, knowing where to sit makes many guests feel more comfortable. Table cards at the entrance to the reception tell your guests where you've seated them. Place cards at the table tell them where to sit.

Some hostesses like to seat people with family or friends they know. Other hostesses like to introduce people with common interests, and they do this with creative seating. Either way is fine. It may seem considerate to seat a cherished aunt or beloved grandparent at the bridal table, but remember that you will be mingling with your guests and not spending lots of time at the table. If there will be other relatives to entertain them at the bride's table your absence won't matter so much. Otherwise, seat them with relatives or their friends, so they are not left sitting alone.

Autumn decorating is simple since everything is bright with color. Even without flowers, this table (opposite), glows with warmth—from the cluster of lighted candles set atop a mirror, the bright berries on graceful branches of bittersweet, and the mellow hues of the leaves used to embellish napkins. Make your seating arrangements bright, too, with rhinestone "candle-jewelry pins" pushed into a pillar candle creating a number for each table. This table décor is elegant and easy to achieve.

Potted seasonal plants in full bloom are an inexpensive and versatile way to achieve color in abundance.

Crisp rows of napkins and a few potted plants create an elegant setting.

NAPKINS

Crisp cotton or linen napkins, in white or a color that complements those you've chosen for the wedding, can be folded many ways to coordinate with your table setting. Colored ribbons, raffia, strings of beads, or bits of lace make simple napkin rings, suitable for any reception.

If you want something more dramatic than ribbons and rosettes, why not use your napkins as surprise packages? If you choose any napkin-folding pattern which gives you a pocket, hidden or not, you can tuck in any number of wonderful little favors and treats, to make the memories last a little longer. Tuck fragrant lavender or rose sachets made of pastel silk into the napkins for ladies, if you have place cards, and sachets of plaid fabric with masculine smelling herbs for the gentlemen's handkerchief drawers. Or make exotic foil envelopes to hold a few candies, and share (chocolate) kisses with all.

Winter simply sparkles. Capture the glitter of ice and snow in a shimmering array of silver vases and julep cups bursting with pale yellow roses. Iridescent glass balls add snowball shine to the blooms of the large bouquet. The bride has arranged seating beforehand, and the identifying number for each table is set into a large silver frame. Tiny silver frames trimmed with inexpensive costume jewelry make elegant, one-of-a-kind favors. All frames are made using the same quick and easy instructions (see page 59.) Silver satin ribbons wrap around simple white napkins—the final touch for this glamorous table.

Dress the tables with paper runners and colored pens, and ask your guests to write their names and best wishes, even some impromptu poetry. Or use an inexpensive tablecloth that can be embroidered for a permanent memento after the reception.

A GUEST BOOK keeps track of guests who attended your reception and is something you can reminisce over long after your wedding. Choose a blank, ruled book—an inexpensive white guest book at a stationery store you can personalize with touches of your bridal colors is ideal. Place it in a location where your guests can't miss it. This is the perfect spot for a gorgeous floral arrangement that will attract the guests' attention. Add a small hand-lettered or printed sign requesting they add personal messages along with their signatures. Ask one person to be in charge of the guest book, so it won't get lost in the shuffle of the general clean-up after the party.

A swirling assortment of ribbons and chiffon turns a plain tablecloth into a flower-topped dessert for the eyes. The hand written menu adds the finishing touch.

As an alternative to a guest book, consider these options:

❧ Provide one large single page that guests can sign. After the wedding transform it into a displayable keepsake by having it matted and framed. (What a great wedding gift idea!)

❧ Place a large glass fishbowl on a flower-filled table, along with a decorative sign requesting your guests to fill out small cards with wishes or advice for you and your new husband. Remind them to add their names.

A PHOTO GALLERY, SLIDE SHOW, OR VIDEO of the bride and groom will entertain and delight your guests. Assemble photographs from your childhood all the way through your courtship in the format you choose. Display photographs with captions on a large easel to greet your guests as they enter the room. Videotaping still photographs in chronological sequence can be compelling and entertaining. Set up a TV screen on or near your guest book table where guests can gather.

FLOWERS AND CANDLES

When selecting flowers for the reception, consider the theme of the wedding bouquets. Or use seasonal flowers for a natural setting and to help control costs. Single-flower centerpieces with their mass of perfect blooms create a strong visual impact. Lilies, roses, daffodils, lilacs, and peonies all look wonderful as single-flower bouquets.

Consider silk rather than fresh flowers in arrangements that you can later use in your home. They will keep colorful memories around you, and you can spice up your wedding décor with a variety of arrangements.

Live plants are also are appropriate for the reception. Pots of tulips, exotic orchids, fragrant hyacinths, even palm trees are available almost anywhere, including supermarkets. Tuck plants into decorative pots or rewrap them in beautiful paper and ribbons. Give them to members of the bridal party when the day is over.

Another alternative to flowers is fruit, plain or sugared, mixed with flowers, mounded into bowls, or hanging enticingly from compotes. Fruits are especially beautiful in fall and winter, when sugar-crusted grapes look like clusters of jewels and brightly colored citrus is plentiful.

Candles speak of warm romance. Clusters of candles with flickering flames create an atmosphere of tenderness and nuance. Not just for evening, candles turn a simple wedding breakfast into a festive affair and add a warm glow to an afternoon tea. Let them brighten a mantel, sideboard, or the guest-book table. Consider borrowing or renting candelabra; if you haven't enough for the entire room, reserve them for the bridal couple's table. Or mass single candles of different heights for a similar effect.

Whimsical bottles autographed by the bride and groom become unusual centerpieces when filled with assorted flowers.

Fresh and colorful potted tulips can be as lovely as an expensive arrangement.

ELEGANT EXTRAS

While decorations for the reception will be concentrated in the main room, where guests spend most of their time, remember to carry your decorating theme through to any extra rooms or spaces guests may visit. Add a few flowers or a potted plant, candles, ribbons or tassels, even a candy dish to the powder room, cloak room, front porch (or if appropriate), the kitchen.

Set the head table apart from the others by decorating it with a larger or fancier bouquet, more candles than on the other tables, perhaps swags of tulle and tiny lights along the edge (see photo right). ✧

Drape tulle around the bride's and groom's chairs (below), securing with generously-sized ribbon bows. A bolt of tulle is the inexpensive way to make just about everything look romantic. Even balloons (right) can be simply elegant when strung together into heart shapes with small lights added for extra sparkle.

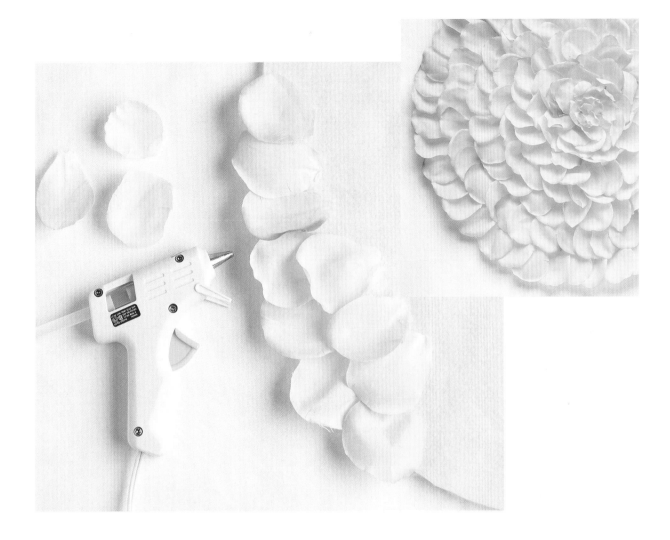

ROSE PETAL TABLE MAT

See the table setting pictured on page 43.

SUPPLIES

8-10 silk roses, each with 5"-6" blooms

20"-square of felt in a coordinating color

Hot glue or craft glue

Compass, scissors

INSTRUCTIONS

1. Make the base of the place mat first: draw an 18"-diameter circle on the felt using a compass. Then adjust the compass and draw a second circle 1" inside the first. Continue drawing circles, each 1" inside the previous one, until you reach the center of the mat.

2. Next, remove the petals from each flower by carefully cutting through the base using scissors. Separate the flower petals according to size. Use larger petals on the outside rows and successively smaller ones as you work your way toward the center.

3. Using the outermost pencil line as a guide, begin gluing the petals to the felt, overlapping each petal to cover about ¼ of the previous petal and extending the first row approximately ½" beyond the edge of the felt.

4. Each new petal row should cover about ¼ of the previous row and should alternate in direction. Continue gluing the petals to the felt base, working your way toward the center fo the mat and using the penciled lines as a guide.

5. When you reach the center of the mat, glue the final round of petals in place to resemble a flower center.

Forever More

Wedding Favors

WEDDINGS TAKE PLACE IN SUCH AN ATMOSPHERE OF JOY and generosity that at many receptions even the guests receive gifts. Bestowing small favors on your guests is a time-honored tradition designed to thank them for taking the time to join you as you celebrate your special day. "Favor" comes from the Middle English "favour," meaning "friendly regard." Isn't that exactly what you would like to convey to your wedding guests?

Some favors, such as chocolates, are intended to be enjoyed immediately. Others—candles, for example—go home with your guests to be savored at leisure. Sachets, bookmarks, frames, or keepsake boxes also can serve as mementos of your happy day.

Plan your favors so they perform "double duty" as part of your reception décor. Keepsake frames make attractive place cards at dinner tables. Ribbon-rose pins work well as napkin ties. Dainty sachets in your chosen bridal colors will brighten up place settings when simply placed atop dinner plates. Cluster candles on a table to greet your guests as they enter the reception hall or sign your guest book. Or, charm your guests by having your flower girl or ring bearer circulate among them with a beribboned favor basket.

Heart-shaped treasure boxes (opposite) provide double delight, first as fetching flower-strewn favors to brighten the reception decor, and second as containers for added gifts such as pastel candy mints or chocolate truffles, potpourri, or other mementos of the festivities.

Traditionally, favors were given to female guests, but today you may bestow them on all your guests if you please. You can purchase favors or create them yourself. If you choose the latter, add up the cost of all materials and multiply that sum by the number of guests for an estimate of the total cost (and to stay within your budget). Also consider the number of hours it will take you to complete them, and plan to finish them in plenty of time before the event.

One delightful way to save time with favor-making is to enlist family and friends to help you. Throw a party and make it an event! Set up a miniature assembly line for multi-step favors and you will have them finished in no time.

You will find a gallery of charming favors on the following pages, along with complete instructions to show you how to make them. Add your own personal touches. Play around with colors and embellishments. Above all, have fun! ᴣ

HEART-SHAPED BOX

SUPPLIES

4"-wide papier-mâché heart-shaped box

4"-square handmade paper

28" of ½"-wide silk or rayon ribbon

1½"-diameter silk rose with leaves

Acrylic paint in two or more colors (aqua and peach used in sample)

Paintbrushes, water container, paper towels

Deckle-edge scissors

White craft glue

INSTRUCTIONS

1. Paint box and lid inside and out (as shown). If desired, paint a sentiment on inside bottom of box (see photo; "Forever More " is shown as a suggestion).

2. Using box lid as a guide, trace heart shape onto wrong side of handmade paper. Cut out using deckle-edge scissors and glue to lid.

3. Positioning ribbon horizontally, glue center of ribbon to underside of lid. When dry, tie ribbon ends into a bow on the top. Notch ribbon ends.

4. Glue bottom of rose atop bow.

5. Fill box as desired.

Small treasures—vintage costume jewelry such as brooches, clip earrings and necklaces—gleaned from thrift stores and garage sales find new life as adornment for inexpensive silver frames you can personalize with a printed message (see table setting, page 49).

JEWELED KEEPSAKE FRAME

SUPPLIES

3¼"-high silver-tone oval frame

8" string of rhinestones or pearls

Additional jewelry piece such as brooch or earring

Jewelry glue such as E6000, tape

Personalized paper insert to fit frame

INSTRUCTIONS

Work in a well-ventilated area.

1. Beginning at frame top, glue string of rhinestones or pearls to glass just inside inner frame edge. If necessary, leave a space at the top of frame, depending on size and shape of jewelry piece to be attached.

2. Glue jewelry piece at top of frame; hold in place with tape until glue dries.

3. Add paper insert.

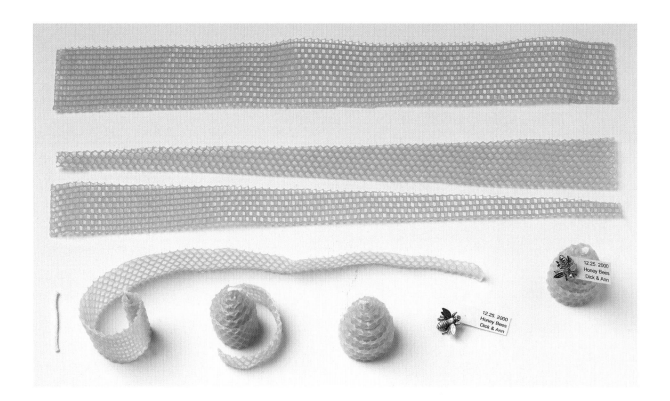

BEESWAX CANDLE

SUPPLIES (these supplies will make 8 favors)

8" x 16" sheet of beeswax

20" length of candle wicking

Eight bee-shaped pushpins

Eight 1½" x ⅞" name and date labels
   (computer-generated)

Craft knife

INSTRUCTIONS

1. Cut beeswax sheet into four 2" x 16" strips.

2. Beginning ½" from one corner, cut each strip diagonally; refer to photo for shape.

3. Cut candle wicking into 2½" lengths.

4. Beginning at wide end, wrap each beeswax strip around wicking, keeping base flat and gently pressing beeswax together at its base as you roll. (Avoid rolling and unrolling if possible.)

5. Attach labels to tops of candles, using a pushpin.

As sweet as honey and fun to make, these "charmed" beehive candles make appealing candle favors for a country-style wedding.

Hand-painted glass votive candleholders bring a fresh and informal look to your reception. You need not be a fine artist to add transparent colors and whimsical polka dots to these inexpensive glass flowerpots-turned-keepsakes.

PAINTED VOTIVE CANDLEHOLDER

SUPPLIES

2⅝"-high clear glass pot (shaped like a flower pot)

Transparent glass paint such as Pebeo®

Isopropyl rubbing alcohol

Flat and pointed paintbrushes

Water container and paper towels

White votive candle

INSTRUCTIONS

1. Clean glass pot using alcohol.

2. Paint rim of pot using the flat brush; let dry.

3. With pointed brush, paint small dots at regular intervals below the rim; let dry.

4. Paint wedding date and names of bride and groom on the underside of pot; let dry.

5. Insert candle.

Poetic sentiments expressed in italic script, tied with a silk ribbon, and sealed with wax create a dreamy, romantic favor befitting a vintage-themed wedding.

SEALING-WAX CANDLE

SUPPLIES

4"-high, 2"-diameter pillar candle

2¼" x 7" strip of decorative paper (wrapping paper or computer-generated)

12" length of ⅛"-wide silk ribbon

Sealing wax candle and metal stamp with floral motif

White craft glue

INSTRUCTIONS

1. Wrap printed paper around the pillar candle, centering it. Trim ends of paper and glue to candle.

2. Tie ribbon around candle, making a bow.

3. Light sealing wax candle and seal bow with sealing wax, allowing a few drops to accumulate before stamping (test first on a scrap of paper).

NAMESAKE CANDLE

SUPPLIES

4"-high, 2"-diameter pillar candle

2¼" x 7" strip of white corrugated paper; ⅝" x 6" strip of decorative paper

2¼" x 2¼" diamond-shaped name and date label (computer-generated)

White craft glue

INSTRUCTIONS

1. Center and wrap corrugated paper around the candle. Trim so overlap is only one or two "ridges" deep. Glue ends of paper to candle.

2. Center decorative paper over corrugated paper and glue in similar manner.

3. Center and glue label opposite the overlap.

Contemporary-looking pillar candles are easy to personalize with an elegant computer typeface, paper in three textures, and a few dabs of glue.

ALMOND BASKET

SUPPLIES

Choose one: Plain heavyweight paper (to print on) or
    4" x 8" heavy wrapping paper

27" length of ⅝"-wide sheer wired ribbon

Glue stick

¼"-diameter hole punch

Paper hole reinforcements

Five Jordan almonds

Sentiment paper with (computer-generated) verse
    (see page 69)

INSTRUCTIONS

1. If using our printed pattern, scan the images on page 69, print out, and cut out. If using wrapping paper, use the image on page 69 as a pattern.

2. Loosely fold paper in half along center fold. Overlap sides of paper into a basket shape and glue in place.

3. Punch four holes where indicated on pattern and apply reinforcements on inside.

4. Following Diagram 1 (page 68), thread ribbon through holes. Notch ribbon ends.

5. Fill basket with almonds.

6. Following Diagram 2 (page 68), draw up ribbon, creating a handle. Tie a half knot on each side (use handle ribbon as part of knot) then tie bows.

7. Tuck the sentiment ribbon into the basket.

A treat of sugared almonds in paper baskets echoes a sweet verse wishing prosperity and happiness for the bride and groom.

DIAGRAM 1

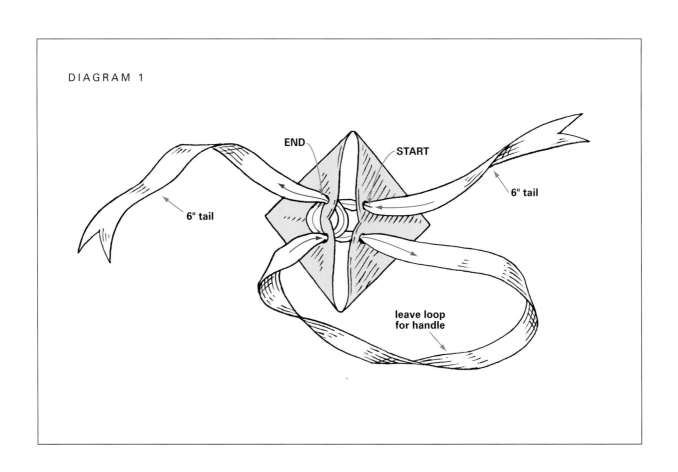

END   START

6" tail

6" tail

leave loop
for handle

DIAGRAM 2

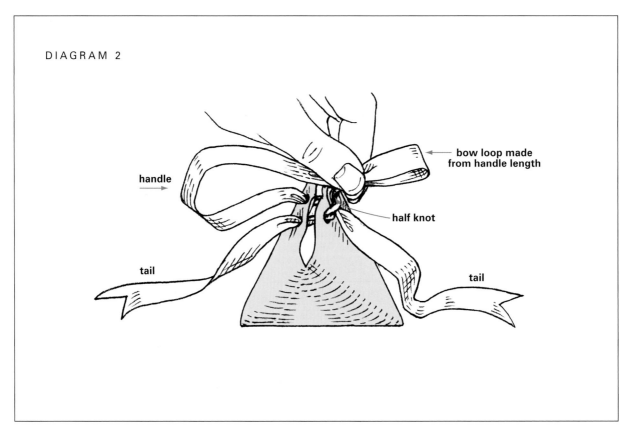

bow loop made
from handle length

handle

half knot

tail

tail

FOLD

FOLD

Five sugared almonds for each guest to eat
Reminds us that life is both bitter and sweet.
Five wishes for the new husband and wife:
Health, wealth, happiness, children and long life.

Five sugared almonds for each guest to eat
Reminds us that life is both bitter and sweet.
Five wishes for the new husband and wife:
Health, wealth, happiness, children and long life.

FOLD

FOLD

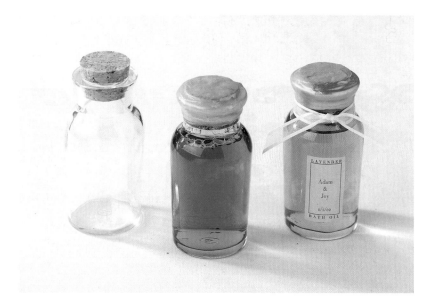

AROMATHERAPY BOTTLE

SUPPLIES

Glass apothecary jar (1¾" diameter, 3¾" high) with cork

Paraffin or candle wax (such as a pillar candle)

Delta Ceramcoat 14K Gold acrylic paint, paintbrush

Double boiler lined with foil (for melting wax)

Scented, colored bath oil or essential oil

10" length of ⅜"-wide sheer woven ribbon

1" x 2" label with names, date, and sentiment
   (computer-generated)

Glue stick

Isopropyl rubbing alcohol

INSTRUCTIONS

1. Wash the jar thoroughly in hot soapy water and rinse well. Dry completely. Fill with bath oil or essential oil of your choice (purchased or made from the following recipe), then seal securely with the cork.

2. Fill bottom of a double boiler with water and set on medium heat. In the top, melt the paraffin or wax. (Because wax is flammable, do not melt it over direct heat.) Melt enough wax to cover the cork and extend below the glass lip of the bottle as you dip it into the pan. Dip three times for good coverage. Let harden.

3. Apply three coats of paint to the top of the waxed top.

The first coat will bead up slightly, but you should be able to get good coverage by the third coat. Let dry.

4. Clean the outside of the bottles with a rag dipped in rubbing alcohol.

5. Glue label to front of bottle.

6. Tie ribbon around the neck of the bottle.

RECIPE FOR ESSENTIAL OIL

Sweet Almond Oil (available at bath stores and health
   food stores)

Essential oil, scent of your choice

1. Determine how much oil you'll need. If the ounces are not marked on the bottles (or if it's in metric), fill with water to the shoulders of the bottle.

2. Pour this into a measuring cup to determine how much each bottle will hold, then multiply this by the number of bottles to determine how much oil you'll need. For example, 100 2-oz. bottles equals 200 oz. For every quart (16 oz.) of sweet almond oil, use 4 teaspoons essential oil. (lavender, rose, lemon verbena, or whatever you like). Shake well.

3. Follow instructions for sealing the bottle (left).

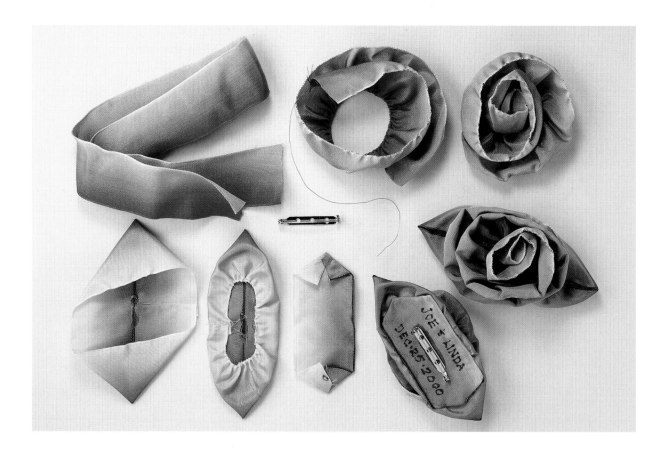

RIBBON ROSE CORSAGE

See also the table setting pictured on page 45.

SUPPLIES

20" length of 1½"-wide ombré wired ribbon for rose

13" length of 1½"-wide ombré wired ribbon for leaves

Needle and thread

Hot-glue gun and "Magic" transparent tape

Needle-nose pliers

For pin only: 1½"-long pin back; jewelry glue such as
  E6000

For napkin tie only (page 45): 12" length of ½"-wide
  ribbon for tie

Optional: permanent, fine-tip marker

INSTRUCTIONS

1. Cut leaf ribbon into 9" (leaves) and 3½" (backing) lengths. On all ribbon pieces (including length for rose), push back fabric on ends of rose ribbon so wires extrude at least ¼"; bend back wires to secure.

2. To make rose, pull up wire on darker edge of rose ribbon to gather it snugly, using pliers. Pull up wire on the opposite edge only slightly. Shape into a rose by folding one short end back 45 degrees and rolling the tightly-gathered edge of the ribbon into a spiral. Fold remaining end back 45 degrees. Secure tightly-gathered edge together using needle and thread or hot-glue gun.

3. To make leaves, overlap ribbon ends and hot-glue together. Fold ribbon as shown in photo and tape inside edges together. Pull up wire on opposite edge (underside) so leaves lie flat.

4. To make backing, fold under corners of the 3½"-long ribbon as shown in photo (center, bottom row). Using hot-glue gun, glue to underside of leaves. If desired, inscribe the names of the bride and groom and the date of wedding using a permanent marker.

5. Hot-glue underside of rose to top of leaves.

6. For pin, center and glue the pin back to backing, using E6000 glue.

7. For napkin tie, center and hot-glue center of tie ribbon to backing.

Take simple lengths of wired ribbon in your chosen color, add a bit of green for leaves and pin backs… and voila! You have classic roses fit for wedding corsages. Amassed, they make a flower bed to greet your guests at the table.

Heart-shaped wire bookmarks will remind your guests of your happy day each time they hear the jingle of the tiny bell charms.

Ring this bell

For all to hear

Our best wishes for

Those so dear.

Names of bride and groom . . .

Date of wedding . . .

WIRE BOOKMARK

SUPPLIES

24" length of 20-gauge Darice Craft Wire

9" length of ³⁄₁₆"-wide satin ribbon

One heart-shaped and two round beads

Two ¼"-diameter silver bells

1½"-square name label (computer-generated)

Hot-glue gun, needle-nose pliers, hole punch

Optional: Wild Wire™ jig

INSTRUCTIONS

1. String bells onto center of wire and twist wire together twice, making sure wire ends are equal in length.

2. Make another twist 2¾" from the Step 1 twists and string round and heart-shaped beads onto both lengths of wire; hot-glue in place.

3. Following pattern (below) bend wire between bells and beads into a heart shape, about 2" wide and 1½" high (see photo), bending the wire twists at the bells to form the notch of the heart. Use a jig for ease and uniformity.

4. Continue twisting both wires together to the ends. Curl end into a coil (see pattern).

5. Punch hole in upper left corner of name label, thread ribbon through hole, and tie into a bow just below beads.

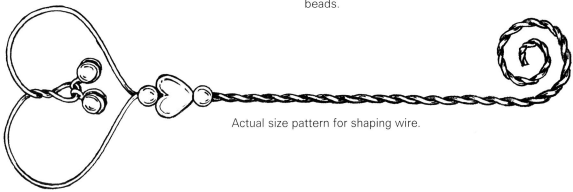

Actual size pattern for shaping wire.

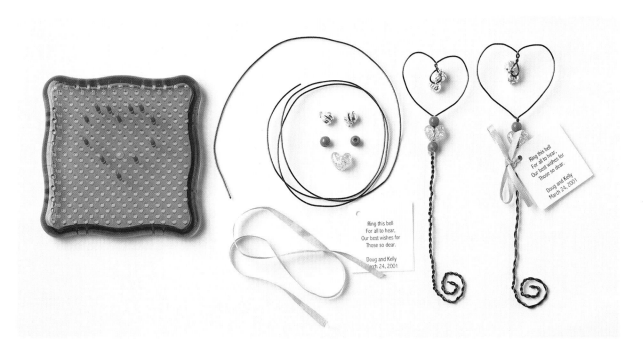

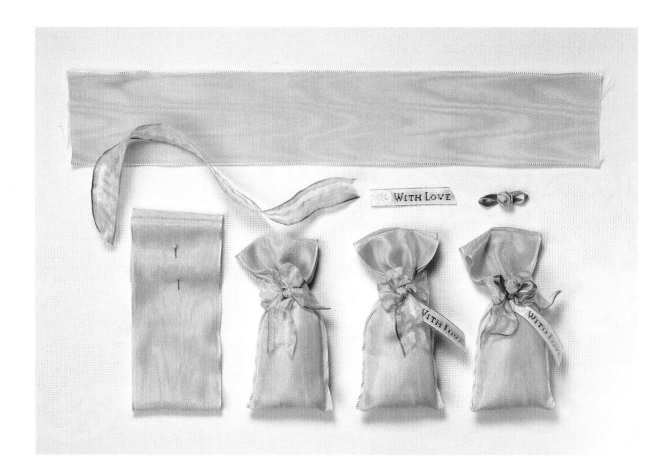

RIBBON SACHET

See also the table setting pictured on page 43.

SUPPLIES

12" length of 2"-wide moiré ribbon for sachet

9" length of ⅝"-wide wired ribbon for bow

Small ribbon rose

2" long sentiment ribbon ('With Love" is shown)

Potpourri

Needle and thread

Straight pins

Optional: hot glue gun

INSTRUCTIONS

1. Fold ends of 2"-wide ribbon under 1", then fold entire length in half with folded ends offset slightly (see photo). Pin in place.

2. Hand- or machine-sew sides of ribbon together as close to edges as possible. Catch raw ends of ribbon in stitching, and secure thread using a small knot.

3. Fill bag with potpourri.

4. Notch ends of wired ribbon and tie a snug bow around neck of bag.

5. Glue or hand-sew ribbon rose atop bow.

6. Trim right end of sentiment ribbon diagonally and glue or sew opposite end just under bow at a 45 degree angle.

Trimmed ribbon sachets make a lovely favor for the ladies on your guest list. With so many beautiful ribbons available now it will be easy to find the perfect shade to duplicate or complement your chosen bridal colors.

BATTENBERG LACE SACHET

SUPPLIES

4"-wide heart-shaped doily with lace border

4" x 3" white organza fabric for backing

14" of ½"-wide rayon ribbon

½"-diameter ribbon rose

⅞"-long gold-tone key charm

White sewing thread

2" x ⅞" name and date label (computer-generated)

Hot glue gun

Potpourri

INSTRUCTIONS

1. Center organza over back of doily. Using short stitch length, machine-sew together along inside fabric edge of doily (use same seamline as lace edging), leaving a small opening for filling. Fill with potpourri (use a chopstick or crochet hook to gently push it into place) and sew opening closed. Trim off outer edges of organza to within ⅛" of seam.

2. Tack charm to inside edge of top "V" of doily.

3. Tie ribbon into a bow and glue ribbon rose to center of the bow.

4. Glue underside of bow to doily just above charm.

5. Notch right side of label. Apply a drop of glue to doily just to the right of bow and attach underside of label.

Battenberg lace, gold charms, ribbon bows and roses dress up white doilies. Filled with potpourri, these romantic sachets are ideal favors for a Victorian-style wedding.

LAVENDER WAND

SUPPLIES

27 fresh lavender stems*, each 14"-16" long

42" of ⅝"-wide wired ribbon

4" length of 20-gauge florist wire

Rubber band

Hot glue gun

Craft scissors or wire cutters, pliers

Bucket or pan for soaking stems

Paper towels

*Different strains of lavender vary in flower size and length. These instructions work best for tall, thin flowers; you may need fewer stems if your flowers are plump.

INSTRUCTIONS

1. Trim leaves from stems. Gather stems together into a bundle just below flowers and tie together tightly using florist wire and pliers.

2. Using a bucket or pan of warm-to-hot water, immerse stem ends of the bundle only as far as the wire tie; do not soak flower heads. Weight the stems underwater if necessary and let soak for at least two hours.

3. Remove bundle from water and pat dry. Holding the bundle with flowers toward you and stems pointing away, gently bend each stem back toward you, pressing each stem with the end of your thumbnail before bending (refer to Diagram 1).

DIAGRAM 1

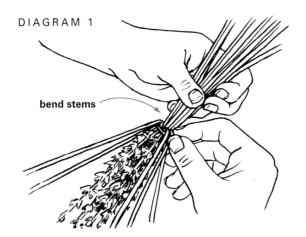

bend stems

4. Using a rubber band, gently secure bundle about 5½" below bend. Allow to dry completely, overnight if possible. When dry, cut off rubber band.

5. Cut ribbon into 16" and 26" lengths. Using the 16" length, slip one end under three stems just below bend (refer to Diagram 2). Dab the ribbon end with hot glue and press stems over it. Begin weaving the ribbon over and under every three stems (if using an even number of stems, use increments of two) in a spiral. Weave to 5" below bend. Wrap ribbon snugly around bundle 5½" from bend and hot-glue in place.

DIAGRAM 2

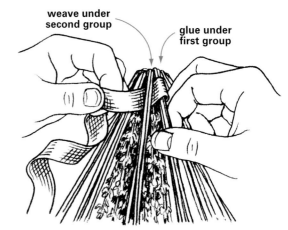

weave under second group

glue under first group

6. Tie the remaining ribbon around the bottom of the weaving and make a bow with 2"-wide loops. Trim tails to 4" and notch ends.

7. Trim stem ends even.

Lavender wands tied with wired ribbon in your chosen color make enchanting favors. Long after the nuptial festivities, your guests will enjoy these fragrant natural sachets in linen, lingerie, or sweater drawers.

Opposite: Sheer, iridescent ribbons and organza, topped with a ribbon rose, show off the petals of potpourri in this keepsake sachet.

ORGANZA SACHET

SUPPLIES

5" x 17" piece of organza fabric for bag

Two 11" lengths of ¼"-wide satin ribbon for drawstring

8" length of 1½"-wide wired ombré ribbon for rose

3" length of 1½"-wide ombré ribbon for leaf

8" length of 1½"-wide iridescent green sheer ribbon for bow

12" length of 1½"-wide iridescent blue sheer ribbon for loop trim

⅞" x 4" label with sentiment, name, and date

Potpourri

Hot glue gun

Needle, thread, straight pins, small safety pin

Scissors, needle-nose pliers

INSTRUCTIONS

1. To make bag, fold fabric with short edges (top) matching; sew side seams. Turn right side out. Fold raw edge to inside of bag, 2" from top edge, and press.

2. To make casing, machine-sew two lines of stitching 1¼" and 1¾" from pressed edge. Cut slits at casing side seams on outside of bag. Using safety pin, insert one drawstring and thread it through entire casing, emerging from the same side you entered. Repeat from opposite side with second drawstring.

3. To make rose, pull up wire on lighter edge of rose ribbon to gather it snugly, using pliers. Fold down the opposite long edge about ¼". Shape into a rose shape by folding one short end back 45 degrees and rolling the tightly-gathered edge of the ribbon into concentric circles. Fold remaining end back 45 degrees. Secure tightly-gathered edge together using a needle and thread or hot glue gun.

4. To make leaf, fold ribbon into a triangle with raw edges even with lighter-colored edges. Pull up wire on lighter edge to gather it snugly. Shape raw edges to match gathered edge and glue to hold in place. When glue is cool, glue raw edges of leaf to underside of rose.

5. To assemble decorative elements, fold raw edges of bow ribbon to meet in center. Pinch together in center (see photo) and hot-glue in place. Glue underside of rose atop bow. Fold loop ribbon by crossing one side over the other (see photo) and secure with a dab of hot glue. Glue underside of bow unit over center of loop and notch loop tails.

6. Hot-glue decorative unit to bag just below casing. Glue left edge of label under rose; notch opposite end.

7. Fill bag with potpourri and pull up drawstrings.

DECORATED JORDAN ALMONDS

SUPPLIES

Jordan almonds in desired shade

Ingredients for each color you mix:

¼ cup meringue powder

½ cup water

4 cups powdered sugar, sifted (for lilies and roses, ½ cup extra for stiffer icing)

Gel food coloring (available at craft stores) in desired shades

Pastry bags, one for each color

Pastry tips:

For violets, #59 for petals, #1 for centers, #349 for leaves

For daisies, #101S for petals, #1 for centers, #65S for leaves

For roses, #101S for petals, #65S for leaves

For lilies, #349 for petals, #14 for centers, #349 for leaves

Flower nails:

For lily, ½" lily nail

For rose, #9 flower nail

INSTRUCTIONS

This project is recommended for those with previous experience with cake decorating. Flowers in order of difficulty (the simplest listed first): violets, daisies, roses, lilies.

1. For each color, one at a time, mix the meringue powder with the water and beat until the mixture forms peaks.

2. Add the sugar, mix completely, making certain there are no lumps.

3. Add the food coloring.

4. Fill pastry bag.

5. Working on a flat surface, form petals, add centers, and allow to dry completely. (Use a lily nail for lilies, a flower nail for roses.)

6. Pipe leaves onto center of Jordan almond and attach the flower back to the still-wet icing.

7. Optional: make tendrils around flowers, using a #1 tip.

Jordan almonds are traditional confections for weddings and bridal showers. Flowers made of royal icing take these almonds a step further, from treat to artwork. If you or someone you know has experience with cake decorating, why not match almonds to your bridal flowers? Novice decorators can try violets, intermediate artists can make daisies, and experts can turn out masterful roses and lilies to surprise and delight the wedding guests.

Memorable Moments

VOWS MAKE THE MARRIAGE, BUT A WEDDING IS SO MUCH more fun with the rings, the veil, and friends and family. The same is true of the reception. Cake and good wishes are enough, but if you want more than the basics there are some updated "traditional extras" to add to the memories.

Music adds another dimension of beauty to your celebration. To accompany dancing or just conversation, music enriches and enraptures wherever it is. And music of all kinds is now more available than ever before. Musicians play every kind of music under the sun, but if they are not under *your* sun, there are disk jockey services to provide whatever music you love, including the sound system, for less than the cost of a live band.

You are not limited to formal wedding portraits, either. You can expand into films and videotapes of the ceremony and the reception, and have them edited into a hauntingly beautiful visual essay of your wedding day, from beginning to end. Technology and tradition have formed lasting bonds to capture the magic, so that you can leave your descendants something more than just a marriage certificate.

A special moment is captured forever in this unusual photo. While on the mezzanine and through a glass partition, our quick thinking photographer created a once in a lifetime image.

Performed by live musicians or sung to a recording, serenades are a favorite way for everyone to celebrate.

CELEBRATING WITH MUSIC

Because a party is usually more casual than most wedding ceremonies, your reception offers you the freedom to choose from a great range of music. Also, you can vary the musical styles and expressions throughout the afternoon or evening. Think about the various age groups that comprise your guests list and what they might enjoy. As a new spin on "something old, something new…" consider a mix of traditional and popular music.

Decide what mood you'd like to set at every stage of the reception. Cool jazz, classical, "soft pop," and romantic "mood" music are all appropriate for receiving guests,

enjoying the cocktail hour, and dinner. Plan to keep the volume at a comfortable level for guests to visit and converse easily with one another.

After the meal is the time for livelier, upbeat music designed to entice your guests onto the dance floor. Save the outrageously loud numbers you love for the later hours of the reception when the younger guests still want to "dance the night away" but the older guests may have left. Discuss all these considerations with your music personnel: disk jockey, bandleader, or the person you place in charge of playing your own pre-recorded music.

Live musicians lend a touch of elegance to the evenings festivities.

Music offers you many opportunities to personalize your reception. The first obvious choice is "your song," a number that has significance for you and your new husband. Next, see if you can find a romantic song that your respective parents loved back at the time they were wed, and play it as a surprise for them. Celebrate your ethnic heritage through your musical selections—something sung in the language of your ancestors, even if it's an old English madrigal—or a dance such as a polka, hora, or tarantella. As you plan the musical selections in advance, make a written note of them and include it later in your guest book or keepsake photo album.

Dancing—whether ballroom, contemporary, folkloric, or country swing—may or may not be appropriate for your reception. Your guest list and time of day will guide you. A small gathering at mid-day or early afternoon, or a reception outdoors, would be lovely and complete with just a string quartet or harpist and no dancing at all.

A LIVE BAND OR ENSEMBLE of musicians offers great entertainment value because it imparts an immediacy and personal touch to the event. As you begin your search for the right group, inquire if you may briefly and discretely drop in at another wedding reception on their schedule to listen to their style and repertoire before you decide.

When musicians take breaks, play pre-recorded music you love that is not in the group's repertoire. Does a friend or family member want to sing or play an instrument in honor of your nuptials? Here is the opportunity for such a heartfelt gesture.

If you feel comfortable with your chosen band and love to sing, ask them to back you up as you sing a favorite song as a tribute to your new spouse, possibly re-writing the words to customize the song. Your guests will love it, and it will be a treasured memory for you, especially if the moment is caught on videotape.

A disc jockey (top) can be every bit as enjoyable as live music. Your special day (above) can be as beautifully preserved as any royal wedding.

A DISK JOCKEY with thousands of songs at his or her command is a good choice for a reception that focuses on dancing. The DJ usually functions as an emcee, so it's important that he or she understands your preferences and the mood of the party you're planning. Check out beforehand that a DJ has the genre of music you want: ballroom, swing, rock (currently popular numbers or golden oldies), R & B, country, hip-hop. Ask in advance for particular favorite numbers you know you will want to hear, so the DJ can have them on hand.

When working with musicians or a DJ, make sure the reception site will have adequate room for the musicians to perform comfortably. Ask them to visit the site to see if it's equipped with what they need in terms of electrical outlets for microphones, instruments, and electronic equipment. Make sure you and your musicians write up a contract specifying what you will get: how many hours of music, how many breaks, as well as all fees spelled out. It's perfectly all right to ask the musicians or DJ what they intend to wear at your reception, so you will know whether it's appropriate for the intended level of formality.

YOUR OWN AUDIO TAPE of personally selected music is a wonderful way to ensure your party will be filled with the music you love the most. With the ability to burn your own CDs now, you can plan many hours of fabulous music. This option works particularly well for smaller, more intimate receptions, especially morning or afternoon events.

See in advance if the reception location has a built-in sound system you can plug into; you will enjoy better sound quality than with a boom box nestled into a corner. Place someone other than your reception director solely in charge of the music, to change tapes or CDs at the appropriate time.

PRESERVING MEMORIES

Documenting your reception party on film, whether in photographs or on video, and keeping a record of guests are ways you can preserve memories to treasure for a lifetime. The camera will capture the moments which fly by all too quickly in the whirl of your excitement.

Photography and videography are ideal for recording the activities that particularly deserve attention: toasts, cutting the cake, the first dance and the dances that immediately follow—father-with-daughter, and mother-with-son, for example. During your reception, take a few moments to assemble and pose with congenial groupings of guests, such as, old school friends or relatives who traveled a distance to attend your wedding. Encourage your guests to pose as they raise their champagne glasses while toasting.

If you want a professional photographer and videographer at your reception, a natural choice is to employ the same individuals you chose for your ceremony. (See our companion books, *Elegant Wedding Ceremonies* and the *Complete Wedding Guide*.) Discuss exactly what you want. Because a reception is not as formally staged as a wedding ceremony, there's more room for leeway, with lots of informal shots that reflect the lighthearted mood of the occasion.

Ask the videographer to "interview" guests and invite them to speak a personal wedding message to you, right into the camera. The results can be priceless! Point out to the videographer ahead of time those guests you absolutely must have on video.

Disposable cameras are fun for your guests and will record for you moments you may have missed. To avoid ending up with photographs that only show guests sitting around their tables, label each camera with an individual "assignment" such as "Take photos of our grandparents,"

"Take photos of children," "Take photos of guests greeting the bride." Instead of placing a disposable camera on each table, consider a basket of cameras on the guest book table, and suggest the amateur photographers return the used film there when they're done shooting. ॐ

Candid photographs of the wedding day will create a timeless present for the bride and groom.

RESOURCES

BAKERIES

MONTCLAIR BAKING COMPANY

Cheryl Lew
2220 Mountain Blvd. #140
Oakland, CA 04611
tel 510-530-8052
fax 510-530-5771
Pages 22, 24, 32, 33, 36,
37 (top right)

LE GATEÂU ÉLÉGANT

Karen Del Bonta
716 Main St.
Martinez, CA 94553
tel 925-313-9076
Pages 30, 35,
37 (top left & bottom), 38

EVELYN SPINDLER

333 N. McDowell Blvd. #A333
Petaluma, CA 94954
tel 707-766-6009
Page 31 (left)

FLOWERS

IMPRESSIONS FLORAL DESIGN GALLERIA

2 Theatre Square, #136
Orinda, CA 94563-3346
tel 925-253-0250
fax 925-253-9946
Pages 50, 52 (right)

THE FLOWER STUDIO

Leslie Hruska
715 Bryant St.
San Francisco, CA 94107
tel 415-536-5905
Pages 5 (second from top), 41

EATWELL FARM

Fresh and dried lavender shipped
anywhere in the contiguous U.S.A.
tel 800-648-9894
website www.lavenderfarm.com
Page 81

RIBBON

MIDORI INC.

708 6th Ave.
Seattle, WA 98109
Wholesale only; call for a store
    near you.
tel 206-282-3595
fax 206-282-3431
www.midoriribbon.com

PHOTO CREDITS

We offer our special thanks to Dianne Woods and to Don Fraser, whose dedication to the art of photography created the incomparable photographs in this book.

Additionally, we want to extend a special thank you to the many brides and grooms whose inspiring images grace our pages.

DIANNE WOODS
1041 Folger St., Berkeley, CA 94710;
510-841-9220

FRONT AND BACK COVERS
PAGES: 5 (third & fourth from top), 22, 24, 30, 31, 32, 33, 35, 36, 37, 38, 43, 45, 47, 49, 50, 52 (bottom right), 55, 56, 57, 58, 59, 60, 61, 62, 63, 64, 65, 66, 67, 70, 71, 72, 73, 74, 75, 76, 77, 78, 79, 81, 82, 83, 84, 85

DON FRASER
1041 Folger St., Berkeley, CA 94710;
510-704-1849

PAGE 4: Mary Jane Pasha and Thomas Maxstadt, Kenwood Inn, Kenwood, CA

PAGE 5: (top) Tracy Richcreek and Dan Sholem, Corinthian Yacht Club, Tiburon, CA; (second from top) Leigh Genser and Chris Mammen, Mira Vista Country Club, El Cerrito, CA

PAGE 6: Michelle Manick and Ken Daxer, Sonoma Golf Club, Sonoma, CA

PAGE 8: Tomiko Iwata and Keith Silverton, Mill Valley Outdoor Art Club

PAGE 9: Melissa Chamberlain and Ken Leet, Clos Pegase Winery, St. Helena, CA

PAGE 10: Heather Dickinson and Grant Fondo, Meadowood Country Club, St. Helena, CA

PAGE 11: Lynn Robie and Geoff Zimmerman, Captain Walsh House, Benicia, CA

PAGE 12: Debra Lewis and Kyle Sullivan, Brazilian Room, Berkeley, CA

PAGE 13: (top) Rose Cardinale and Salvatore Ingrande, San Mateo, CA

PAGE 14: (right) Tomiko Iwata and Keith Silverton, Mill Valley Outdoor Art Club, Mill Valley, CA

PAGE 15: (top) Yvette Carlascio and John Prichard, Jr., St. Francis Yacht Club, San Francisco, CA; (bottom) Julie Skidmore and John Lewman, Fremont, CA

PAGE 16: Carina Quezada and John Peterson, Coleman House, Sonoma, CA

PAGE 17: (both) Mary Jane Pasha and Thomas Maxstadt, Kenwood Inn, Kenwood, CA

PAGE 18: Jody Wrath and Andrew Palmigiano, San Rafael, CA

PAGE 19: Mary Jane Pasha and Thomas Maxstadt, Kenwood Inn, Kenwood, CA

PAGE 23: Mary Jane Pasha and Thomas Maxstadt, Kenwood Inn, Kenwood, CA

PAGE 25: Erica Ginsberg and Mike Kuerbis, UC Faculty Club, Berkeley, CA

PAGE 26: Shawn Elliott and Jack Marshall, Beaulieu Gardens, Rutherford, CA

PAGE 27: Shawn Elliott and Jack Marshall, Beaulieu Gardens, Rutherford, CA

PAGE 28: Tracy Richcreek and Dan Sholem, Corinthian Yacht Club, Tiburon, CA

PAGE 29: Irene Taylor and Ron Edson, Elliston Winery, Sunol, CA

PAGE 34: Tracy Richcreek and Dan Sholem, Corinthian Yacht Club, Tiburon, CA

PAGE 40: Mia Senior and Chris Unterman, San Rafael, CA

PAGE 41: Leigh Genser and Chris Mammen, Mira Vista Country Club, El Cerrito, CA

PAGE 42: Mary Jane Pasha and Thomas Maxstadt, Kenwood Inn, Kenwood, CA

PAGE 44: Mary Jane Pasha and Thomas Maxstadt, Kenwood Inn, Kenwood, CA

PAGE 46: (left) Debra Lewis and Kyle Sullivan, Brazilian Room, Berkeley, CA; (right) Kristina Truitt and Jeremy Taylor, San Dominico, San Rafael, CA

PAGE 48: (both) Mia Senior and Chris Unterman, San Rafael, CA

PAGE 51: Tomiko Iwata and Keith Silverton, Mill Valley Indoor Art Club, Mill Valley, CA

PAGE 52: (left) Janet Green and Charlie Feick, Marin Art and Garden Center, Ross, CA

PAGE 53: Mary Jane Pasha and Thomas Maxstadt, Kenwood Inn, Kenwood, CA

PAGE 54: (left) Cindy Fontana and Bill Kolb, Hacienda de las Flores, Moraga, CA; (right) Angela Simpson and David Roof, Heather Farms, Walnut Creek, CA

PAGE 86: Stacey Getz and Robert Kertsman, Lark Creek Inn, Larkspur, CA

PAGE 87: Janice Johnson and Thomas Savidge, City Club, San Francisco, CA

PAGE 88: Mary Jane Pasha and Thomas Maxstadt, Kenwood Inn, Kenwood, CA

PAGE 89: Jill Foster and Kurt Wharton, The Bellevue Club, Oakland, CA (Lee Waterman Band named Shake, Albany, CA)

PAGE 90: (top) Carina Quezada and John Peterson, Coleman House, Sonoma, CA; (bottom) Virginia Varni and Paul Ratto, Orinda Country Club, Orinda, CA

PAGE 91: Stacey Getz and Robert Kertsman, Lark Creek Inn, Larkspur, CA

DOUGLAS E. SWAGER
Hercules, CA

PAGE 13: (bottom) Deanna Gengler and Matthew Sheehan, Scott's Restaurant, Oakland, CA

INDEX